SO-AKW-757

FARM
TO
FABLE

*A Journey of Life
Through Poetry*

For Trish
Happy Painting
Tim 8·1·2017

TIM CUSICK

ISBN: 978-0-692-79352-7

Tim Cusick
12407 NW Skyline Blvd
Portland, OR 97231
Email: timothycusick65@gmail.com

Ordering Information: Please contact distribution at (503)708-0669.

Book Design, Photo and Art by Tim Cusick

Printed in the United States of America

CONTENTS

Love and Family

Margaret's Bun   3
Reeds Under Starlight   4
Sudafed Letter   5
The Kindred   6
The Puzzle Piece   7
The Walk   8
While You Are Gone   9
An Evening Together   10
Glow   11
The Sound Of Apron Strings Falling   12
The Habit Of You   13
Garryowen To Ballyferriter   14
Pictures   15
Newcomers   16

Grieving And Losses

Caprice   21
Colors of the Day   22
Sadness Plumbed   23
Barbara   24
The Swing   26
New Friends   27
Officer Waibel Died   28
Rodney King   29
For Friends Only   30
Her Best   31
To Papuza The Lonely Gypsy   32
Regrets   33

Farm Life Reflections

Windmill   37
Roostertails   38
Prairie Winds And Irish Spirits   39
Near The Road   40
Never Gonna Farm   41
Picking Time   42
Lying Fallow   43
Serial Dreams   44

On Writing

Hello In There   47
Zero Zip Nada   48
Poetry And Cows   49

Good Morning Glory

The Morning After   53
A Water Song   54
Blue Picture With Orchids   55
Cosmic Quiz   56
Hale-Bopp & Black Coffee   57
Pogonip   58
Sunshine On The Equinox   59
Without The Words Of Night   60
Harlequins, Coral and Fire   62
Coyote Mama   63
Moon   64
Thistle   66
Bird   67
Shimmering Lights   69
Green Dancers   70
Devout Insect   71
Raspberry   72
Summers First Day   73

Diggings

The Myth Of Me   77
Slipping Shadow   78
A Wager Of Neglect   79
Ask Me   80
In My Lifetime   81
Interim Reply   82
Place   83
Shall I Aim For Accuracy?   84
The Walls Of My Cave   85
A Life Of Meaning   86
A Word For It   87
Fairness Choices Habits   88
Sorting It Out   89

Pickle Heads

Playground Helpers   94
The Ashland City Band   95
Double Dog Dare You   96
Bundled Up   97
Distractions at the Comfort Inn   98
Vivaldi After a Couple Scotches   100
First Time Buyer   101
Beyond Today   102
All We Like Sheep   103

Testosterone Happens

My Sordid Affair   107
The Man From The Fourth Street Florist   108
Of Course I Can   112
Snapdragons   113
Hearing Voices   114
Old Dog Dreams   115
The Difference   116
Pretenders   117
A Man Turns Sixty   119
If You Were From Mars   120
The Deal   123
Silly Season Frames   124

Spiritual Echoes

The Sabbath   127
Storm   128
Certainty Lost   129
Earth Climber   130
Gentle Vision   131
Novel But Was It A Crime   132
The Rebel   133
Softies   134
What To Expect   136

Preface

Poems can reveal more than we intend about ourselves. Though my purpose is to share, my inner editor wants to avoid over-exposure. I have attempted to resist him and to be honest about life, however inconsistent the result might seem. I ask the reader to pardon any failings in this respect; and imagine they are part of a salad of greens with colorful vegetables and a few cracked peppercorns. Poetry allows us to share inner worlds, and lets us grow as we examine life on the wing.

I grew up in the fifties and sixties on a farm in South Dakota. That experience shaped me, as did being the eldest in a large Catholic family. As a young adult I noticed my parent's grief about us as they believed they had broken a chain of transmitting their own and their parents' values and creeds. They and their immigrant ancestors found life's purposes could be found near the field, village and church. I suspect the immigrant's great dream was to leave these three strands forever to their posterity. For a couple of generations this vision held fast. But beginning with my generation the world changed fast.

Times change and we change. Today I live on a small farm on the outskirts of Portland, Oregon. I am no more from Ireland than my children are from a farm near Vermillion. But I am from Dakota. Years later I still sport a spiritual farmer's tan from those days. My rich bittersweet Dakota youth underscores for me that parents get the last laugh. They transplant more walk and more talk than they could have imagined. In many ways we are their creatures. When you're young this can be scary. In time it could become an honor.

A hope lurks in me that someday my children will understand the sacred and profane within me, value the perspective of my times, feel the marvelous rhythms of the old farm, and come into my world of natural wonder. Like millions in my generation who left the farm, I accept the fact I have not passed to my children my own tools let alone those carried on the old John Deere. They have the tools that fit their lives today. So while I might hope I passed on my hard learned lessons to spare them a similar setback, life does not work that way.

Many of the voices I use in this collection are voices I heard. I lean to accessibility in my work and hope to sidestep foggy code from one angst filled traveler to another. These poems were written for myself and crafted for simplicity if not simply. Many are light but a few are hard and deadly serious. Some are uncomfortable but important.

For thirty years I was a real estate broker on the west coast. Some writers start with writers' workshops or degrees in English. Mine starts with writing ad copy for my business to make the phone ring. The tightness that ad writing required led me to writing poetry.

FARM TO FABLE is the grown up version of a much smaller collection published to share with friends and family called *A KID IN YOUR CAP*. Many of these poems are fables or written from a naïve point of view. I discourse with plants, animals, moon and stars. This collection includes the usual themes: love and grief, reflection, pain, laughter, play and grappling with angels over time. They were written over a span of thirty years and embrace people of all ages.

I thank my wife Suzanne for her great love and for her encouragement throughout this project. Also a big shout-out to mentors Dean Ing and John Thomsen for their friendship and nudging. Finally, a belated thank you and apology to the English teachers who made my papers bleed.

Tim Cusick

LOVE AND FAMILY

Margaret's Bun

It was two-thirty on a morning back in sixty-four
And we met in the small hall between our bedrooms
She stood robed with hair over both shoulders
Light from a street lamp formed a silhouette of her body
Silver sparkled in her hair as she faced me
She turned, and I could see that it streamed
From her crown to her waist.
This was the only glimpse I recall
Of grandmother with her hair down
And the first time I realized how beautiful she was,
As a woman, that is.

Reeds Under Starlight

Star bright, twinkling eye
Beyond all but my heart
Lifted to yours with memories
Of lonely places and lovely passions
Searching the heavens
You are isolated for your brilliance
Briny tears glisten in the darkness
Empty voids beyond your beauty
Echo softly after your song
By day blue sky remembers your signature
Your heart is gathered in creation's tapestry
Teasing winds sculpt textures into your garden.
And I wait for you among the reeds
Swaying as your marvelous life
Enfolds us in great light
I feel the pull of your power
and as the greater absorbs the lessor
I am drawn toward you now and forever.

Sudafed Letter

Thanks to a five pm Sudafed at two am
I sweep the kitchen and empty wastebaskets.
Then a hot chocolate sweetens my wait for the muse.
The silence enlarges the memory of a quiet ride
Taking you to the airport, a week of small talk
Done…over…like a deathwatch. I keep silent.
I associate the quiet with you.

Down to the basement I oil a squeaky furnace damper
It's intermittent banging interrupted the solitude
Nagging at me as if a list of honey-do projects.

I love living here. It is a gift we give to each other.
You sounded well by phone this morning
Your many unknowables revealed
Your experience with silence brings me comfort
Rain threatens with light wind and finally comes.
I cancel the afternoon open house.
Spoiled plans shadow me closer than old Jake.

The Kindred

See, they're walking again
Not hand in hand
If you watch closer
They're heart to heart
Confessing and sharing
In deep quick code
What they can about
The heart of the matter
Now softened with teases
Encouraged by smiles
Their balmy spirits are hurriedly
Discovering gaps and closing them.

The Puzzle Piece

Cleaning out our daughter's room
I found a puzzle piece under the bed
That was covered with fuzz and sticky old dust
Which I swept into the center of the room

An unceremonious task parents do
When a kid heads off to college.
I found pennies, hairpins, but the puzzle piece
I put into my pocket for no clear reason.

I felt it in my pocket the rest of the day
Until it was time to go to bed; and the
Shoebox in my drawer where I keep change
Gained a few coins, but the puzzle piece

I recognized from a snowy Christmas Day.
I held in in my hand for a close look and a rub.
It was from a puzzle that resembled a fishing village
In Norway with vast fjords, blue mountains and a boat.

That particular puzzle had five hundred pieces
We spent hours and hours putting it together
The picture on the box was deceptively simple
Our house was full of laughter, and lots of fun.

That Christmas was a winter wonderland and the
Kids careened wildly on their saucer sleds down the hill.
Tonight I muse about an old puzzle piece still in the shoebox
And remember kids away at school.

The Walk

She walks with me and for a time
We listen to crunching gravel beneath our feet
She looks to see if our neighbors are home
I notice a gopher mound and decide to set a trap
She speaks about expelling a kid from school
Who had been caught with a knife
I catch myself, somewhat alarmed
Though I am accustomed to her stories.
The first time I was terrified,
The risk, the danger, the guilt I felt
She faced a dangerous situation.
The fear has faded for her if not the risk
But I think: a false move, a bad trip, a desperate child
Neurons banging out of control, arms flailing in rage,
She presented the knife at the expulsion hearing
To a parent in denial, distressed, yet instinctively
Defending the cub like a sow bear.
She says it gets easier
But yesterday I saw the sixteen-inch knife
Honed steel, a Japanese model so sharp you could shave.
Four finger slots for gripping the handle like brass knuckles
With a drawing hook below, and lethal ripping edge above.
The gravel snaps and pops under our boots
The fresh clean air in my lungs feels good.
I notice her tired slight limp
As we turn onto a lane toward a nearby construction site.
We cluck about a neighbor with eighteen TV sets
And a master bedroom larger than the houses he builds,
Whose ego seems larger than his bloated house.
I mutter hollow epithets
Till his ears should burst into flames.
Up a long steep grade both puffing a little
We turn onto another gravel lane that chatters amiably.
We exchange news from the kids
Ambling past roses dozing along our driveway
She ticks off her list and I go for a trap.

:

While You Are Gone

The bed holds my body and diffused mind
In her Saturday grip as I ignore daylight, and the dog
Then it releases me to answer the phone.
You know the drill: In a blue robe I step outside
As Jake recaptures his kingdom. A gray day,
Low clouds buzz our humble castle
And spatter us with mean little droplets of rain.
Breakfast is a sloppy concoction of Cheerios
Granola, semi-frozen strawberries, sugar and milk.

At the office my business had mirrored the weather
So I select and bind a small collection of poems
For the reception of poet Linda Gregg.
Later, as the rain and wind increase,
I pick my way through files of receipts and dreams
Without any major finds except the
Peace of mind I get from knowing where things are.

I wage an energetic war against clutter in the kitchen.
The quiet destroys my usual notions about time alone.
I think of you. I head off to the reception as if it matters.
I'm not a social lion among strangers and
Disappointed I depart early leaving my poems
For the guest of honor puffing cigarettes on a porch.
I come home, feeling silly.

An Evening Together

Coming home at night
Is the best time for me
Especially when she is there.
Tonight she met me at the door,
With a kiss,
And her bright smile.

Jake was there too, as usual,
Wriggling and squirming
Jumping and licking.
I felt grungy from the day,
So I went to the kitchen sink
And washed my hands.

We enjoyed dinner at the table
With stuffed pork chops, and
Asparagus, one of my favorites,
With a glass of red wine.
It was the first night off
For both of us in some time.

Our hearts were grateful,
And we had fun. We laughed.
We were kids once
And we had fun together,
Just like now, yes
Just like now.

Glow

After many years returning
Home after dark far too often
The warm light in the window
Lifts my soul, for I know
She loves me after all.

The Sound Of Apron Strings Falling

Give me a hug and kiss before you go
I'm going to miss your soft touch, and searching blue eyes.
Become an adult and swing headlong into the task
Boldly bring your un-tempered beliefs to the hot forge of life.

Furiously pound them with hammer of iron, test them
Let brave notes sound from your throat, bite bitter tears
Curve and sway with the resolve of a tough tamarack
Bracing for winter wind under hooded black skies.

Don't turn back, you have important times ahead
So sift and sack, save or ruin. Just persist and
Come full circle if you like, after you've found your own rock.
At our front step a little stone frog will wait for your return.

The Habit Of You

There was a moment when my promise to be with you
Became a habit, and a nearer moment when the habit
Of you became an addiction. Oh, how I do love thee.
Like a cigarette, enough to satisfy my craving
Enough to spend my last dollar buying you flowers
Enough to choose being with you over all else.

I remember you caught me snitching a cigarette on the patio
You asked, "Have you ever thought about just quitting?"
My ears rang for three days and my arms tingled up to my elbows.
This is day five since you left. I didn't know love could be an addiction.
My brain washes me in wavy endorphins
When I am with you.

Perhaps I have an addictive personality
Because craving and I are seldom apart.
Indulging myself in you I lost myself. In your absence I am listless.
My ears are not ringing nor my hands tingling I feel
Just dullness. I wonder if my personality needs to give itself
To whatever or whoever will take me.

I've seen how alcohol addictions
Can be insidious, permeating all: relationships play and work.
Every choice directed by a liquid god.
Is an elixir of love any different?
Without any real effort or intention
You seeped into the cracks of my life and I became rummy.

But while you are gone I am drying out.
I placed a seal between addictive love and my habit of you.
My habit of you will be richer for us both if I displace you
From some of these crevices and recover my life.
Going cold turkey is scary, like when I quit cigarettes.
Did you know about my problem?

Garryowen To Balliferriter

I stand with mom
At the headstone
Of Tim O'Connor
Her grandfather
And my namesake.
The old immigrant
Is buried on this prairie Not far
From an abandoned church
In Garryowen.
His adopted homeland In Dakota
Is vast and windy Like Ireland
Spare of trees.
I never met him
But my mom and I
Stand with our hands
On the stone marker
As dad snaps our photo.
We are proud to be
At this place together
It's windy and brome grasses wave
In their season
As do we.
A stone hovel stands here
At the birthplace of
Great Grandpa Tim
Close to Sligo Bay
I slog through smelly runoff
From the dairy
Behind the house a dirty brook
To snap a picture
To take a better look.
A few kilometers down the road
Is a stone church Garryowen
Tim, we're told, was baptized here
Our guide is cousin Denis
A near copy of my own granddad.
We kneel and pray at Mass
My son is uneasy
We move on beyond the Oratorio
To the graves of our kin
Some of them still three hundred years.

14

Pictures

Old pictures on the wall
Parents, grandparents, all
Frozen in a flash, with
Their unsung races complete.
I am uneasy
They seem so resolute and sure,
Unyielding, they haunt me:
We did it, you can too.
They make life so simple
These pictures trapped in time
They never fail or flinch while
I unerringly fail and quake.

Yet I do know of them
That they failed just like me,
And if per chance they did not,
Their lives were hopeless frauds.
O dear God,
If by chance or fate,
I become trapped,
A picture on the wall,
Let the tragedy and the glory
Of my life never hurt
Or ring with eternal pride.
Let me bequeath a gentle side.

Pictures on the wall
Should be rotated
To protect descendants from this fate
And my critic from unneeded cruelty.
Harsh judgments as these
No one should deserve.

Newcomers

We walked the property yesterday
With a plot map and a compass
Beginning at a stake in the northeast corner
Near the house.
I fussed with the compass long enough
To correct for magnetic north,
And we headed west
Along the neighbor's wheat field.
Two hundred feet from the house
Beyond the garden where the woods began
I discovered a conifer had fallen
Into the woods toward its kind.
It was the one with a fork
About forty feet up that
Grew two tops and one
Had become a snag.
That particular Doug Fir
Had a twenty-four inch diameter,
Rotten on the inside
And home to thousands of beetles.
I remember watching a crow last summer
Sitting on the snag and being sassy
Who scolded me while I pulled beets
Someone else had planted.

We stomped north a hundred feet
Into the neighbors wheat field to
Help us get around a huge stand
Of blackberries that was impassable.
This is where Jakes' sagging jaw,
Could no longer carry the ball;
Or when he became caught up
In a more exciting adventure.
Three hundred thirty feet later
Suzanne reached an electric fence,
Which she assumed was not hot,
It shocked her twice.

Five hundred feet from the comer,
We headed south returning to the property line,
Where we found a surveyors bleached ribbon
Tied to a birch of some kind.
We were now in a mixed forest
And heading west again down into a ravine,
Filled with towering evergreens
And dense with sword ferns.
Soon we were in a completely different world
Like a rain forest, which of course it was,
With rotting logs at our feet and brush,
That complicate our many efforts to stay on line.
Ahead of us Suzanne heard trickling water
We have found the headwaters of the ravine,
Crossing over the little stream
About fifty feet we found the pin.
Emboldened, our trio headed south
Down into an incredibly steep ravine,
Plotting our course by compass
Noting distinctive trees as our markers.
Carefully picking our way down the hill
We found two deep well-like structures
One of mortared brick, the other concrete
Both were covered with heavy lids.
We had heard about the spring on this parcel
That provided water for the old homestead
Located a quarter mile below our house
But we could not find it in the lush summertime.
Like kids opening presents we continued south
Covering the five hundred feet along the west line.

We paused occasionally to view the sights
That were astounding to our eyes.
We encountered another fence
Which we easily stepped over,
Except for Jake who suffered
A barb to his maleness.
Checking our compass bearing first
We headed east where we joined a path
Most recently travelled by a herd of elk
That migrates through here every winter.

17

Crossing over the stream again
We are at the lowest point on the property,
And heading up the wildlife trail where
The old logging trail winds up toward the house.
Just before we break out of the woods,
I notice black scat at my feet,
Of a carnivore, which I assume
Is from the bobcat or one of the coyotes.
Jake and I had seen the bobcat hunting in the pasture
The day before and it ran down that trail
Into the woods to avoid
A barking dog who needs no introduction.

Where the logging trail emerges into the pasture
We found the electric fence on our property
Has been trammeled by the elk
Who must find people troublesome.
Determined to walk the property lines
We headed into the pasture and down the fence
A few yards repositioning ourselves to where
We think the south line picks up again.
Marching upward and eastward across the pasture
We find the south fence line of the neighbor;
And we continue our course to the southeast comer
Of what we call 'our place'.

Invigorated by the adventure and happy
Jake and Suzanne head toward the house,
Both bit by fences;
And I wait, winded from the climb.
Back at the house now I put down the map and compass
Jake recovers his ball and is hosed down.
I laugh, because the absurd purpose of our adventure
Was to place a value on the land.

GRIEVING AND LOSSES

Caprice

You might come here Sunday on a whim
If the sky is blue and we get enough wind
We'll fly kites in the pasture
So bring Icarus and Daedalus
I will put my new delta into the stratosphere
And you can do the same.

And if it is a sunny windless day
We'll make our escape and watch songbirds
Teach fledglings to fly or feisty hummingbirds
Thrust and parry in gallant duels over sugar-water
Or red tail hawks test ailerons as thy hunt.
In the garden there are raspberries bursting with fruit
And snapping pole beans aching to be picked.

O that my ache could be plucked so easily
Or dashed in a flight to the sun
As I contend with remembering and forgetting
The wide-open smiles and taunting grins
Snatching from us the artful rhythms of her life.

Today I walked into an aromatic cathedral
Of cedar, fir, musty needles and rotting twigs
And sat on a fallen tree trunk and sighed
I listened to the blurps and gurgling promises
Of the creek to carry my troubles to the sea
It is a spirited place and it lifted me up.

If the day is otherwise pleasant
We can go to this marvelous place and sit
To let go of our remembering and forgetting
Or exchange them in the marketplace of wonder
For the beauty of the day.

If you do come here Sunday, on a whim
We'll make our escape into the heavens
We'll run and touch the earth with our hands and feet
We'll be brave and have a ceremony in the woods
Taking time for remembering and forgetting.

Colors Of The Day

I stand at the door today looking outside
At the drab December sky. Bare trees
Are stripped of their fiery splendor.
Leaves drape their trunks like a pall
And grumble about the coming winter.
It is a day caught between seasons,
Dreary. The colors of the day are
Mauve, gray and a dull lavender.
My eyes are misty and my brow hurts
Then I realize this day is part of life.

Sadness Plumbed

Sunshine
Your silence is deafening
Your pain does not leave me
O lonely contrarian
The beautiful joys could have been yours
Swallowed whole in isolation.

Barbara

If I had an hour with you,
I would tell you I love you.
I would not try to make sense of life,
But I would thank you for being my friend.

I would thank you for being my sister.
I would listen intently hearing your every word.
And of course I would hug you close,
And I would hold your hand.
I would tell you that I was afraid,
And I would cry desperately.
I would thank you for being a friend to us,

But I would also laugh with you about childhood times,
Adventures in the ravine,
Picking mulberries and throwing eggs.
About walking home from school,
And going to the swimming pool.

I'd admit the really dumb things I did,
I'd say you're special and that I admire,
How you lived life without pretense or a facade,
How you honored the child and remained playful,
Always ready to have fun.

I'd praise you for the friends you kept,
For clear passion for justice and doing the right thing
I'd tell you that your compassion was a healing balm.
I'd laugh and tell you that you were amazing and outrageous,
That I've never met anyone so impractical,
You'd get kudos too, for running your race without balancing
A checkbook, and ignoring the inconsistencies of life
Following a road map that was in your heart.

I'd celebrate your achievements,
With your husband, your daughters and your son.
I'd ask about your paintings that hang all around;
I'd claim credit for teaching you to color on walls.

We'd do duets; songs we sang before.
And I'd comment on the courageous life you lived.
I'd ask if you knew we had been by your side,
In my desperation, I'd tell you again that I love you.

The Swing

There is a swing
At an old school ground in Modesto
With a horse suspended by chains
And a yellow bee on a spring.

The young woman recalled
Being there as a child
Today she took a sad little boy there
Hand in hand though they were strangers.

And with her mom she walked beside the boy
Whose mother died two days ago
The area has changed, she said.

It seems unsafe.
Do you remember, I came here alone
At his age my sister in tow?
No one comes alone to this playground.

Her mom watched as her daughter
And the boy took to the swings
One with the boy, but she felt grief
On their first trip here together.

They pumped and pulled
Yelling at the sky
In peals of joy, one louder than the other
Though the young woman was twenty.

While walking back
The young women
Talked to the boy without a mom,
Her mother lost in thought.

New Friends

Met new friends today. At least
I hoped they would become friends
But their eyes plainly spoke of pain
Anger and grief. Pain was evident
Dissolving, regrouping, flickering and leaping
Grief bowed their heads in turn.
Maybe they will not be friends of mine after all
They met a new friend today.

Officer Waibel Died

i say that just once wherever they are
we meet to form a line of respect
a thousand of us to a cop and one at a time
we thank them
we shake their hands
we tell them we love them
and we give them a hug
sear it into their minds
brand it onto their hearts
three hundred million citizens
respecting our men and women in blue
we and they bound into a real us
they would be overwhelmed
and confident in our love
we would transform america
including our trash
we might even help the rest of the world.

Rodney King

Fifteen minutes was all it took.
The news capsulized you in seconds
You cried to the world
 "Can't we all get along?"
Maybe the LA cops were goons.
Maybe you were loaded.
And the high-speed chase wasn't a good idea.

But in that great moment of clarity,
When you said those words
Why did you cry?
You approached us with truth
"Can't we all get along?"
You lost your voice
Some people laughed.
Late night comics got new material.

Though some white folk felt convicted then
You did enormous good.
You simply asked the penetrating question
And it crawled under our bright skin
And kept crawling and crawling
Like a shiny foxtail
How we itched.
Oh how we itched.

I'm told you went back to a hazy life.
The heartfelt moment passed.
For a time the gulf widened between us
Your desperate cry for an answer died
Your great question was no longer on the table.
I think I knew why you cried.
America should have too.
Sorry Rodney.

For Friends Only

Have you ever looked at a friend to confirm
Some action was the right thing to do?
Have you noticed how support from a friend
Comes quickly as options diminish?

There is a racing to close in on the crisis
Provide flapping wings to help it fly
In a rush to somehow share the unequal loss
A radical choice whether your breast, my prostate.

Then after the private bargain: ok, take a piece of flesh
But let me have time with my friend
Let me review all those easy times
When my soul was not desperate.

I recall a time when a friend's advice
Helped me transcended my selfish anger.
Have you ever looked to that kind of friend?
When fear and a metallic taste was palpable?

Her Best

Jeanette who is twelve and looks her best
In red braids and pert wire rimmed glasses
Is pretty but her bright open face has a secret
She cannot tell because she is ashamed.

Her older step-brother came home one night
When her Mom and Dad were gone and
Taking her down, he stripped her
Of her pajamas in one powerful sweep.

He slapped her face till it was red and
Persuaded to lie still without screaming
Blood trickled from the side of her mouth
Hot snot salted her lips, and her wrists were red.

He screamed she was a dirty little slut
That it was time for her to learn some lessons
He placed a kitchen knife to her nostril
Ordering her to undo his pants.

She did her best sitting as he stood
His other hand twisting her braids
The little child with small budding nipples
And a dozen pubic hairs shuddered.

Shaking all over, struggling with his jeans
She voided her bladder when his smelly cock
Rose from a shiny endless sea of hair.
He twisted her hair again and again.

Madness had its way that night,
In addition to musky tastes and smells, she was
Destroyed, and with sticky drying on her thighs
Jeanette did her best and agreed never to tell.

To Papuza The Lonely Gypsy

No one understands me
Only the forest standing alone
And the river, tired and unable to crest its bank

So too I follow the course of my mind
Twisting and turning like you
Changing with the seasons of life
Running together yet standing apart.

Cursed by the accursed, drifting along the bayous
Living on catfish and talking to kingfishers.

No one understands me
Cast out from among outcasts
So my own words became companions
For a lonely heart.

Words that echo among haunted trees
Or babble in my hoary head as if
Water splashing over a cold stone.

Regrets

I wish there were more sooner
Had my armor been less thick
Perhaps the blade
Might have reached me quick
With a rush of color
The message that I needed to change.

But please, before you speak
Ignore the impulse to rush
To invalidate my tardy regrets
And for now tend your own, please.

FARM LIFE REFLECTIONS

Windmill

At the first breeze you creak,
 Followed by a long screech.
Your motor moans and I lean against
Your warm, galvanized leg.
Cattle's ears are easily cocked,
On these calm, thirsty, mirage-like days
When algae hangs drying on the musty
Innards of your round wooden tank.
All eyes turn upward at the flash
Of your sleek, silvery fins and watch
As the long, slow pull on the cable lifts
Your stem with clang and scrape.
Cows pause in the pasture, then break
Into a run, bellowing toward your tank.
I climb upon the pipe pulling steel
To help a weak wind lift your load.
Dear breeze, please persist
That we may drink the water
You tease up through the pipe
It is a very old, spontaneous prayer.
Faster wind and cranking motor
Plunging stem and running water,
Excite the assembled hearts now
Beating to the sounds of your work.
You were a cranky but intrepid friend
You stood watch night and day
Ever ready to catch any soft wind
And spin your soulful moods to all.
Now your legs are stretched and stacked
Beside rusting old angle iron of no further use.
A motor took your job, if not your place
And I touch cold bones I once knew well.

Roostertails

The Midwest was hot that summer,
There is a patch of sand by the Missouri
We planted to drought resistant corn
Scorching by July the weeds still grew.
That day I had finished cuttin' hay
And took the mower off the tractor
By the lower bayou next to the tank.
Seems to me they were both dry.
Scraped my knuckles mounting the cultivator,
But heading down to that corn field
I held the throttle wide open, with
My tennis shoe tugging at the governor.
Made quite a rooster tail as I blasted
Down that dusty road thinking
Maybe me and the Johnnie Popper
Should race Bobby Joe and his Case.
The sun poured out its wrath all day
Blisters on my nose were oozing and
Above my naked waist I glowed ember red,
The sunscreen protection was dust and grease.
Being down there seems distant now.
A gallon jug wrapped in burlap,
Soaked in the tank carried in the toolbox.
It was tepid as bathwater before noon.
The only person I recall seeing then
Was Mom who brought lunch, a smile
Soft words of kindness, our shared concern
The entire field would burn before it tasseled.
I recall I sang my lungs out to the poppa chuffa,
Poppa chuffa, pop! of our old John Deere B
I watched heat waves dance late in the day
Billowing with mounds of gnats.
Round about eight it started to cool, and the
Old Deere was puffing now to a breeze while
I watched for signs up by the timber for a rooster tail
Chasing Dad in his old blue pickup.

Prairie Winds And Irish Spirits

A granite cross and small stones
Mark Irish-American graves
On this flat windy plain in Dakota
Half a mile from an old wooden
Church called Garryowen.
Where the folks were married and I was baptized
Now a dusty antique store on a near treeless plain.

But back in Ballyferriter this man
Was baptized in a stone church
Where Mass is still said daily, twice on Sunday.

The strong winds continually combing the prairie
No doubt reminded him of Hibernia because
I recall the unrelenting winds of Dingle Bay
Kept my son's glorious, red hair
Aloft like a flag.

Prairie winds were a balmy friend to the immigrant
Except in winter when they were a furious enemy
Howling ceaselessly as he squat in a sod hut
Wrapped in a heavy coat and hat eating smoke
From cow chips between puffs on his pipe.

I imagine the native grasses laughing
At the audacity of O'Connor and friends named Merrigan
Lynch, Ballard, and Manning as they tried to skin
The prairie and plant up to her potholes.
Today grasses bend solemnly and Irish spirits linger.

Near The Road

Two barns were raised together, standing
A thousand feet apart; and just two hundred feet
From what had been a century ago,
A rut between two farms.

Serpentine rock delivered by a glacier were
Used as cornerstones; and cottonwood lumber
Cut and milled nearby, was pulled by
Puffing mules, then pierced by thick nails.

Only God knows the number of calves
Born, cows milked, dreams realized
Or lost, the whiskey bottles drained,
Hid or found by kids or scolding wives.

And how much hay was lifted and piled
High in the mow; and how many first kisses
were shared; or if these barns ached when
Young men left and never looked back.

Today the rut is a highway, no farmhouses
Remain, and the two homesteaders
Names are unknown, except to a couple
Laughing cribbage players at the home.

Fruit trees, lilacs, and daffodils watch as
Wild blackberries snake around these relics
As if to spring; but now to mourn, because
A shearing wind leveled them last night.

Yes, on the same day they fell. Can
You see what is happening? In a moment
We can stop the car, and look.
They are becoming dirt again, together.

Never Gonna Farm

There are tough times in farming
Really! Are there times that aren't?
Farming seemed a metaphor for loss.
Yet farmers don't have a lock on suffering
Bitter farm hardships stand behind
The Indian, Jew and Black, frequent adversity.
Destination myth, extinction or the past
Still no honor endured or sought.
Shared by young and old, some hot some cold.

Trips across the fields erased by hail: Black and white.
Or Dad standing on a frozen bluff, looking, his thoughts
To himself, seldom spoken yet clearly sensed.
I count baby lambs taken
Last night. Untimely births: Black and white.
Frozen stiff Dad, I counted them.
There's a calf below the bluff, too bad.

Didn't count the farm auctions but
We usually bought something: Black and white.
The place is full of weeds. Run down huh?
Gonna' stop at Grandpa's? I wanna buy a lemon pop.
You could not count the grasshoppers.
Beans were full of them: Black and white.
Soon November's corning and the picker will be on.
Just about deer season, ain't it Dad?

To the man God said this garden
Shall be to you as a curse. Why Eden's sand!
Sure farmers lose but they tend to blame
Nature, cattle prices, the bank or Washington.
See, my eyes are dry and my cheeks feel hot
There is no black and white.
Can't I blame somebody, something,
Surely not me. It hurts Dad. Do you understand?

Picking Time

First geese of the year
Flying south to beat the storm
Honking, flapping quickly and
Falling leaves the grove adorn.
There are signs winter is here,
Hurried fractals in early light,
Sundogs suspended on the western sky
Gotta get another load in tonight.
Blackbirds on the swarm
All day now from early mom
And the corn isn't picked,
And the cattle aren't fed.

Lying Fallow

Spring was a northwest kind of wet
Muck sucking at your heels
And without being cold
It was too cool for most garden seeds.

My garden took the year off
A sabbatical for self-enrichment
A node of nitrogen here and there
Under the legumes that braved the bog.

My life is like that sometimes
I shut down
Without knowing or admitting it
Till my God half the year is gone.

I don't understand rest
Anymore than I understand why the wind
Wears itself out late in the afternoon
After hot goldfinches have called it a day.

Though I rest quiet time makes me uneasy
As if someone or something is passing me by
Time can be spent but not saved
A perishable that cannot be bought or sold.

Today I talked to my sleeping garden
As if a friend I hadn't seen for a spell
Watched my words drift away and peter out
As if the wind went to there and stopped.

When the garden lies fallow it dreams
And like my mind it grows weeds
If it cannot produce some kind of crop
Today we dreamt about spinach and beans.

Serial Dreams

In the dreams I went back
Though I know you can't
For several nights I did.
We live at my parents' farm raising our family
Same wife, same kids, continuity drops by
There is a warm festive ambience as if
All are given a new beginning in an old place.
The scene is sweet and astringent as a dead ripe peach.
Like no other these seem real because it is
Backlit by another dream long gone yet
Now in reach and illuminated by the sequel.

I work at a promising job at an oil company
Our move back is complete and I have an easy commute.
I don't milk cows or cultivate corn anymore
But somehow I am home
Possibly doing the victory lap of an adult child
Even though everybody knows
You can't go back.

I live in a world of ebb and flow
Of cycles, some easy, some hard
Contending with three dimensions and time
Making the best choices I know how
Experiencing the commons
I'm following through with the stuff of life
And wrestling with old angels.

But as the dreams weave together
They become surreal because of each other
Coupled together in vibrancy
I awake and stumble to the bathroom
Would they stand the test of dreams and
Fade into some misty place in the brain?
Evaporate as ether?

Now I sit in bed with my first cup of coffee
The images have a residual quality
More movie than dream
The farmhouse was sold many years ago
There wasn't an oil company in a hundred miles.
The kids are gone, and this isn't South Dakota.

ON WRITING

Hello In There!

Where are the words that came pouring out
Splashing onto the paper?
From bioelectric synapses to perfectly ordered little soldiers
Brave erect glyphs ready to endure obscurity
Or fiery and piercing bloodshot eyes
Or fade to yellow over time?

Has it all been said by Shakespeare
The Victoria Falls of wordsmiths?

Yesterday the words were here and they
Tumbled like little gymnasts
Tapping in my skull seeking to escape
Any hole before the light dimmed.

Where are the triggers to let them loose
To frame the page,
To come forward as my servants?

Into the vapor perhaps gone forever
Leaving me to grope about in the dark
Seeking candle and a match.

Zero Zip Nada

A burst of words should explode onto the screen
But they don't and those that come are a grudging
Motley brigand of pseudo-thoughts scuffling, quarreling
Littering the landscape who then traipse off. I let them go
I lower the needle that spears, sifts and threads
Them into a left-handed sort of order.
They aren't strong so I will deny them from reaching paper
I listen for an hour to the banging protests
Of their tinny tiny drums.
I wait them out trusting them to march off the screen
Or toss themselves into a bottomless digital canyon.
It is the best I can do. They do and I have no remorse
A blank white screen page is more pleasing
Than a scrappy burst of unappreciative words.

Poetry And Cows

You wait for a stray to swagger by
Drift in or even stagger and fall
The plan is to catch one
A phrase without a subject
So you can swallow it
And ruminate like a cow
.
Let the hay lay in your belly and
Scratch your innards while
You lie down in the pasture
Catch a few winks
Convert long wave to short
Roll the eyes and hum

Bat flies
The muse sees you breathing
And is drawn to our side
Deep down in your viscera
Comes a little burp from the cud
Pith for contemplation
You chew quietly.

In the gust of a summer breeze
You swallow again.

GOOD MORNING GLORY

The Morning After

Warm drizzle fell straight from heaven
Not wavering on this perfect still morning
A slug, newly hatched poked along the rim
Of an orange peel in the compost.
Wild blackberry and sycamores had set their buds.

I followed the garden path to the woods edge
And peered into the leafless trees awash in moss
Still dancing were the large wet ferns
Splayed about from too much drink.

I chopped through the blackberry thicket
Resolving to restore and then extend a path.
Felled branches are strewn as if giant confetti
A downed tree requires a saw to clear.

Looking about this seemingly unhurried place
Nothing seemed more urgent that being there
In the drizzle,
In the moment.

A Water Song

I make my way
To you
Whispering past your door
To give you life
And now I rush
Back to the sea
But
I leave you singing firs
Reaching for the sky painter
Who colors your canopy
Pink and blue.

Dazzling spots of
Light
Shimmer against me
In the moss and leaves of trillium and fern
I glisten
Off boughs, chanterelles and feathers.

Let the sun embrace you
And draw me deeply into your lungs
Watch and I will wrap you in a blanket
Of mist
Or gallop past you circling the mountain
On plumed and billowing steeds.

Do come
Come to my sanctuary
Where you can spend your days
In awe
Where you can rest
Where you can merely be.

Blue Pitcher With Orchids

A blue and white ceramic china pitcher depicts a harmonious
An imaginary village. Round mountain behind, good feng shui,
Honored ancestors give them good luck, make them rich.
It is a temporary home to less lucky orchids,
Their deep green leaves swarming like corn and upright
Ending in snaky spikes with craning necks
And twelve frightened flowers each with a tongue
Caught in a gagging reflex their faces deep pink becoming violet
As if from an asthmatic attack, twelve comics
Their jeers stalled in a coughing fit
Bewildered to be placed in a milk pitcher and surrounded
By the plodding of Chopin's Marche Funebre: Lento.
Cause for concern but we are companions tonight.

They with pleading eyes and earnest smiles:
Can we trust him? Does he care?
I return their gaze with a thin apprehensive smile,
Like the first time I was asked to change a diaper.
They seem patient and forgiving. I wonder if they are strong.
I must do something for they are unbalanced
Out of place in the pitcher, in need of better feng shui.

Cosmic Quiz

What if life is a relay race
And the team that finishes first
Is the team that learns last
Life was not really a race;
And for any team to win it must
Have done whatever it took
To ensure all the teams
Could finish?

Hale-Bopp And Black Coffee

Sunday morning and Bach sliders awake with black coffee
To slake the Portland gray sky du jour. Bright Hale-Bopp
Barrels past us and should return next in year 4385.
But tonight's celestial fuss, an acorn lunar eclipse,
is at risk from cloud cover.
Coyote Mama came into the yard today – healthy
Still favoring her right front paw but hunting.

Shamelessly I scored a brownie mix from the cupboard
Baked it for my open house summoning a childhood skill.
Today's focus is doing what I can---not what I cannot.
Three dry days yet asthma keeps me from cutting the lawn
I think of trying today and going slowly.
I think of by-gone friendships, people I'd love to see.

Loneliness is a poor companion.
I saw two mutes having coffee
Chatting amiably with busy hands and
Cloistered monks their canon of vespers
And Gregorian Chants
You called and sound invigorated a pin number away from a power day.
The kids are great. The youngest capitulated with a phone call.
Hopes are up for a terrific open house today.

Pogonip

Their shiny eyes poke into the formless pale
Our vistas reduced to claustrophobic dread
White curtains blanket the west and
Creep through valleys in broad streams weeks at a time.

Pogonip grips us one by one, house to house
We shudder, not against Jove but the bleak,
I listen to swooshing sound of the bold in cars
Boring light channels, hope for the others.

Our gazes mimic statues draped in thick ice
As though life will be numb till the sun shines
We peer into nothingness from our pedestals.
Mourning doves laugh, tuck faces in down.

Sunshine On The Equinox

In Portland it can rain so long her inhabitants cease to believe
In the sun. Yesterday an associate challenged me
To rise at five-thirty this morning and stand an egg on it's end
Because it will balance on its head during the equinox. Right.

Much ink had been given to a comet visible in the northeast
Before dawn and the northwest after nightfall. Show me.
The sun burst through the clouds and stayed with us all day
And last night when I let the dog out I saw a huge comet, a comet
That has not passed this foolish place in four thousand years.
Now I must wait another year to stand an egg on its head.

Without The Words Of Night

Do you recall the silence of midnight
When there was nothing left to do,
Except explore in cool lapping of moonlight
Imponderable wonders shut out by day?
Some vestige of ancient ritual past
Followed me into a den of city lights, I am
Facing the moon through a window screen
Looming as if at a talking machine.
Entranced by deepening shades of blue, watching
Black become a color again; and a child-like squint
Creates moonbeam magic with a golden shaft.
What color are the trees in deep night tint?
Do you recall reflecting on reflected light
Which had moments before been chased by darkness?
And silence yielded to the sounds of midnight
Leaves were carried... by an undulating breeze?
The conductor of the cricket orchestra was gone
Endless tuning but never tuned. Arrhythmic
Night bird calls, cries and fight .... so
No more than music do words depict the night.

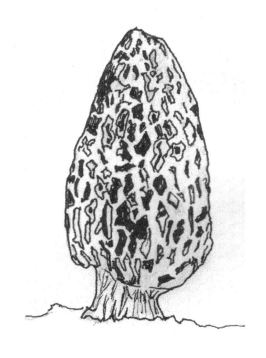

Harlequins Coral and Fire

Huge dragon like curls of smoke engorge the valley
And the sun, a sorry has-been fallen from Broadway
To Vaudeville, reduces its light to a dull orange
Bored, serving shadowy daubs of light to blackened natives.
Charred spears and naked firs from Silver Creek,
Kalmiopsis and elsewhere cackle while
Perform grim battle with their smoking branches
Raised like the wooden swords of a million harlequins.

September's fiery walls triggered natures slumbering spores
We know in our minds May will bring
Jillions of rhizomes contacting one another
To quietly conspire beneath a forest floor of ash.
Not an offer of verse but obverse
'The fire is terrible
No, the fire is not terrible
There are morels, say again
No, there are not no morels
Come May please come May.'

Springs sloping warmth qualifies hopes
We pass sceptics near barbershop poles
That morels are pretty well picked over
Josef and I wink, then we'll search for chestnuts!
Bound by our love of morels
We negotiate the tortured hillsides
Sooty feet finding tenancy
In the tracks of the terrible infidels who came before.
Two men find delight in sunny places
Snatching joy from the sprigs of green
Perennials of hope that follow every war
New to us but old ways of seeing.
Apocalyptic gleaners searching.
Josef scans the ash, bends to inspect, and I watch, learning
Our sharp jackknives cut the corals of the forest
From time to time we lean against giant charred skeletons.

Coyote Mama

What happened to your paw, Coyote Mama?
You can't catch gophers for your pups.
You were hunting the pasture last evening,
So slow you couldn't win a three legged race.
Coyote Mama, your pups are hungry,
Stayed where you left them, down by a tree,
But instead of playing they watched you
As you slowly hopped round the field.
Did you get all Krueger's chickens last year?
It doesn't matter now, with no easy meal
Two miles of here. Hey! Coyote Mama,
Can you nab some shrews, or snag a mouse?
Crows are laughing, the cat's not scared,
A half grown calf chased you away.
Were you bit, kicked or step in a trap?
Could it have been, a hen house nail?
Where's your man Willie, Coyote Mama?
He can help or you'd think he would,
You're getting skinny and looking pretty sad
And the gophers will be here if you mend.
We heard pups howling last night Mama,
And I wonder if their stomachs are empty.
Your man Willie, he showed and hunted the field
So did a pup, whose best wasn't good enough.

When Mama was gone more than a week
She was seen again down in the pasture
Hopping, hopping, skillfully catching gophers
While her sad paw flapped like a rag doll.
That night the coyotes sang like an antiphonal choir
From the lowest places in the ravine to the highest
There were young voices and old voices alike
Eerily celebrating the return of Coyote Mama.

Moon

The man in the moon blinked,
Yes, I saw him, yes I did.
"T'was hard to get your attention" he gasped,
As the wind blew away his stash!
"Time was you know, I was
The only show in town, show in town.
But let's not talk about me mate,
Let's talk about you.
Wot the devil you clowns a'doin' anyway?"
His bushy eyebrows bristled through
The atmosphere and they too drifted away,
As if to catch the stash.
"Nothing really" I blurted, startled not believing,
I looked left then right, "Am I insane?"
More quietly now, "Nothing really ... sir,
I remember when you really were
The only show in town
Show in town."

Thistle

You're a superstar Thistle, and that is the problem.
You propagated from a tiny, almost imperceptible seed
Into a dark green thief devouring light and space.
We've talked about it, and in a word, you don't fit in.

Bees like your pollen, and flamboyant butterflies
Slurp your nectar, while stuffed larvae roam your leaves;
And frankly, your blue flowers are pretty.
But thistles aren't team players, and that's a problem.

Thistle, you are obnoxious, even to other weeds.
There's been talk in the field and around the garden.
You don't have many friends, do you?
What's this? This is a hoe, Thistle.
Let me show you how it works.

Bird

Bird, does anyone talk to you
And do you know anything about life?
I like you,
You seem to understand the seasons
Of life, and what to do next.
They say that your brain
Is hardwired
Though there must be a more elegant
Way of putting it.
It seems
Nearly impossible
That you could be so beautiful
And so perfectly matched
To your world or
That such an exquisite creature
As yourself
Could perform so well with such
A tiny brain, and yet you do marvelous things
Like build nests, fly, migrate
Raise babies and teach them to fly.
Bird, you seem to always have the heart
To sing
For lots of apparent reasons
And some that are not so obvious
Such as it pleases you.
It seems you have something to teach us
When we observe your ways.
Your wisdom bird,
Even if it is built into you and
Not acquired,
Has served you for as long as
Our kinds have shared the earth together.
You are industrious, and efficient
In all your ways.
I can see you are not one for introspection
Which may be
Something else we could model.

You live peaceably,
Oh,
I have seen you squabble
Over territory, we do that too,
And you certainly have your pecking orders
But I must say I have never
Seen you go to war.
Bird, you are not all business either
Because I have seen you
Time and time again
Take to the swift streams of air
And play motionlessly suspended
Tilting your wings to let the wind
Lift you out of sight and from my perspective soar
Straight up, as if you were taking an elevator
To the clouds.
They say your kind is wise enough
To know the hand of Saint Francis from a crush you.
How do you do that little bird?
Can you teach it to your babies?
Can you teach it to our babies,
Or to me?
Bird, does anyone else talk to you
Bribe you with seeds
And pry from you the secrets of life?

Shimmering Lights

They say January is unseasonably cold.
This year is also dry and the winds
From the Columbia gorge have howled
Till their voices are hoarse.
Tonight there is not a cloud in the sky,
From our house I can see far
Across the valley where glittery lights
Seem to shimmy as I shiver.

Green Dancers

Garlic sprouts, red clover, blue grass, pink carnations
And oak tree dancers: Grab your partner, circle to the left,
Cells circle to the right, push down for water, reach up for sun
Mitochondrion waves rocking and rolling around the globe.

Chlorophyll factories building lush green fractals
Coded to thrive, while below molecules remind
Synchronized swimmers that form follows function,
Roots reach, hairs lift water and minerals anchoring the shaft

Trickster hormones seduce cascading flowers to come forward
To be beautiful and attract bees and hummingbirds
Natures sex toys who begin the foreplay.
I'll take the blond and you take the redhead,

Oooh! I got sticky on my head
Buzz off! Buzz On! Buzz off again, but buzz often.
The seeds are growing and my bulb's enlarging!
I don't feel pretty. Oh but you are and I love you.

Devout Insect

Let me tell you about meeting a Praying Mantis:
I'm serious, he was on his way to church;
Since I had attended the ten o'clock service,
I thought he was late, but I couldn't be sure.
He was dressed in brown looking his best.
But the little fool blended right into the asphalt,
and I almost blended him into the sole
Of one of my best go to meeting shoes.
I gave him a lift to the lawn,
Which was halfway to the church,
No, he didn't say thanks.
It's so typical these days.

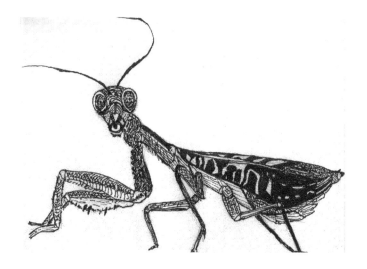

Raspberry

Wake up canes, from winter's death,
Spring is coming, let's celebrate,
And I will remove your spent twigs
Tying and clumping the quick stems
So they arch as if blowing in the wind.
You will feel the warm sun and the flow
Of sap through your veins.

Summer's First Day

Sunshine
And every living thing is
Singing
It's own kind of song and my own
Spirit
Is lifted in the joy that
Summer
Is here and winters dark
Solstice
Cannot be farther from me than
Today.
So I rose this morning at
Light
To begin my celebration as early as
Possible.
Birds singing.
In the northeast a thin crest of the
Moon
Is lit by a slow advancing
Sun
Beyond the distant arc of the
Earth
The brightest day of the year begins.
Festivities
Are afoot for all creation in the
Hemisphere
This summer I am giddy with
Joy
That fair opiate of the heart's
Desire.

DIGGINGS

The Myth Of Me

The first time I became a man
I did not know I was a myth
Cast into roles I made for myself
From flesh, bone, brain, desire, and ego

The first time I became a man
I believed in myself and my purpose
Vaguely adult in the cool consistency
Of paste clasping the veneer

The first time I became a man
The certainty of my power was my power
The power of conviction my formidable ally
I did not know I could fail as I recall
The first time I became a man
My mind was uncluttered by procrastination
And I was awash in a sea of opportunity
There was certainty I would realize my dreams

The first time I became a man
The myth of me became a legend
My will gave honor to my beliefs
I was master of my destiny
The first time I became a man
I did not know how to pick myself up
Because I had never fallen down
I was authentic as an unrestrained child

The last time I became a man
I tried to recall the myth
I hoped to find the pieces
To direct the rest of my life

The last time I became a man
I found everything had changed
My flesh, bone, brain, desire and ego
The veneer was gone and I was vulnerable

The last time I became a man
I was more thoughtful, reflective
Life was more precious as if
I had one more chance to get it right
The last time I became a man
I was cast in the role of a child
Self-conscious and filled with wonder
Asking questions, taking it all in.

Slipping Shadow

Shadow died or found another
When I transparently left him
Clutter and other things that owned me
Which for years he wanted.
Mornings were hell with Shadow along
I could not step into the light
Without him shuffling in by my side
I howled at the day he found me.
By noon he grew short ever
Under my feet, bleating, bleating
That he let me step on Shadow
For my own good so he said.
He was more grotesque after lunch
And despite his short twisted limbs
He kept up even as I lengthened
My stride trying to shake him.
I treated Shadow with scorn and contempt
And warning my companions to avoid him
I promised them that someday soon
When he grew weary, I would be free.
He gained energy all afternoon and
He often overtook me in piercing hot sun
Grinning and gloating about his power
At nightfall he would slip away
To sample lilac nights and dewy pleasures
Among pubs, restaurants and holes
Where he reveled without me.
However he managed to rise and meet me
Though he lacked substance
He fed voraciously on me, gnawing my soul
Smacking cold lips with alien pleasure.
At last I reasoned he would die without me
So with effort I became transparent
Wrenching free I left things that owned me.
He must have died or found another.

A Wager Of Neglect

In my heart where justice and injustice are
Gathered together,
Stored up
And Saved,
There is a vague area where Mischief goes
To count, keep score and dig into old sutures
Near the large cauldron
Over the flame controlled with two buttons

            Like me
            Unlike me.

Around this large workshop
I place sentinels, mangy dogs of neglect,
To preserve and protect
The things I gather together,
Store up
And save.
Some dogs I starve for love, food or greatness,
Others work full time to magnify, focus and harness
My pedestrian fears with lies.

One is more vain than a gypsy bovine
Who compresses his herd into a circle
And dispenses the role of dominance and horn.
I note an ancient air about him as he
Gathers together,
Stores up and sets aside.

Standing next to Justices' cranky waterwheel
Behind the Vulcan's workshop.
Is Genius, Mischief's smarter brother,
Together in charge of cataclysm.

I'll bet if you could add scarcity, a famine
Or take away a few toys to excite them,
One of them would push the wrong button.

Ask Me

(After William Stafford *Ask Me*)

Some time when the river is ice
Ask me again how my life has changed
Ask as well about the difference
Between being a dog or a coyote
Or about following the trail of others
Ask me if given the chance, would I do it again?

If the ice is thick enough we will walk up the river
And listen to it crack and moan beneath our feet
As waters caught between ooze and ice
Silently obey the whims of the channel.
We will look for rabbits along the frozen bank
Till our feet and ankles are numb
If you ask me again I will answer.

In My Lifetime

Fifty-five miles per hour, and the traffic
Is painfully slow on the main highway
It moves like a Slinky, and drivers seem short
On patience along route two-seventeen

It is my secret impulse to speed up
Pull back on the steering wheel
Lift off and bank toward home
It seems the reasonable thing to do

I can feel gentle pressure on my fingers
Against the wheel as I free myself
From gravity and a frustrated world
It is an impulse that won't go away.

Interim Reply

You ask how I fare
Some intensity in your eye
And after the pat response
You get a pensive stare.

I think you might hear
Conviction with a startled cry
Scurry over rusty synaptic cables
Like strumming piano wires
To a dusty spot reality seeks
Solace however cryptic
However fleeting.

Thank you for shifting your gaze
As an inner mute is shaken and
Although he began to stir
Is still unable to find a word
Or frame a thought as
The stasis of life floats away.

Your question runs deep
Horning it's way into a place
No mirror has been
I have not found the answer still
The one you ask
Nor one to share.

The mute and critic are disturbed
And for now there is no better answer
To how I fare.

Place

The search intensified
Now that I look back
To just before I faced the fact
I am a creature with a definite
Sense of self and place
My restlessness was a permanent address
Into which I sought entry
My place my reality

And now, having found
That comfortable place
Former residences are more
Clearly seen for what they were
Perhaps here I will learn
Those places were touchstones
Or more precisely road signs
Prompting me to

Move on to a quiet place
Listen to my own voice
And stay there
Perhaps there is more.

Shall I Aim For Accuracy?

Shall I aim for accuracy
To express who I am today?
Ought I improve on the past
Shake the burrs of error and clay?
Can I merely say past is past?

So too there can be no who
When a smug present
Does not stir or reach
Even in small furtive ways
For who I am is not precisely who I was.

Shall contentment displace merely being?
I cannot perfect what I am not.
Tension pulls up the slack
Forget revisions but accept the core.
Part of me, the greater part of me

Rises to declare I am who I am.
For life brought me this far
Continuing to smooth and polish
Thus I am who I am
Without deceit, pride or equivocation.

The Walls of My Cave

So then
Let me begin
With a clear purpose
Let me slip into the cold stream
Of consciousness bravely flowing
Forever toward an unknown future
As if I were confident I could come back
To the world unchanged like
A cave dweller returning
If you will, to a seasonal cave.

The bones suggest
As do the paintings on the walls
We have been coming here for ten thousand years
Or for as long as we have known the moon
Though I have exchanged emerald rains
For the safety and ease of civilization
I still think I can go back and it will be the same.

But something is out of place
As I look at the ancient stones on the garden path
Outside the walls of my home and pause
I stumble on the word purpose:
Purpose?
Yes I have a purpose for my life
Sometimes fuzzy about the particulars
But I am sure the answer is related
To the remote technology in my hand.

A Life of Meaning

The head of a fool pursues
The meaning of life.
He has no clear answer for
He has a poor question.
And invested it with much time
As he circles a turnstile
Like an ox treading grain.

But how about a life of meaning?
For me it is love expressed tangibly
Helping myself and family
To see, know and experience
Good, healthy, positive and possible
Broadcasting the fun of life.
Anything less is cheating life.

A Word For It

Apprehensive, a word stuck between the head
And stomach
Where butterflies flutter into a formation
From the panic of trying to catch a plane
Queuing up in one place
And realizing you should be in the other.
Or being frightfully lost yet thought to be a native
By a local seeking directions.
A word that answers pleading eyes among lovers
Help me now
If you love me there will be no fear in the spaces
Between us, give me assurance or another word for it
Everything is OK
Even though we both know it is not always so.
Apprehensive as the cry of a child after the story is told
And the lights go out
'You won't leave me till I'm asleep
Will you, you ask, Mommy or Daddy
Whoever you are
Every night, but they do
After they say they will be right here
And you extract
A promise they will leave the door open
A little ways, at least till the dreams begin
And you navigate the seas
Of yet another night and when morning comes
You are brave again
And join everyone for breakfast.
There must also be a word a widow knows loneliness
And reading her name on a stone
Without a date she hears him whisper softly
Like he's done before
"You won't be gone long, will you?"
Just as there must be a toast that parents use
At weddings for everyone
That assuages fears and builds hope.

Fairness Choices Habits

If you think life should be fair, God help us.
It is not, and if it seems to be so, things
Are not as they seem.
If you think you get what you deserve,
Life will be harsh. You get what you get
And that is all.
There are many simple choices in life,
One of them is procrastination,
Another is happiness,
Living life's choices is not a choice.

Sorting It Out

What to do?
Shall I serve or be served?
Grasp or release?
Conquer or surrender?
Laugh or cry?
Win or lose?
Love or be loved?
Answer or question?
How shall I live? And
How shall I exchange
The times of my life?
A creature with the time
And space to carry on
With life's choices.
Perhaps with the gift of time
And space I shall have the will
To gain wisdom and make
The choices of an old man
Who could do it again.

PICKLEHEADS

Playground Helpers

Tumble from the stream of children
Flowing onto the playground yard
As if sand filling an hour glass
Happy screams rumble feet run
Over the field of fun an alluvial fan
Pressing the limits of glee.
They swarm over the structures
Thick as ants over a split orange.

From among a dozen 'whatcha doins'
Four little helpers ascend
Ladder and climbers to the highest deck.
"I'm gonna help" "Can I help?"
"I wanna watch" and "Me too"
Three girls and a boy
Peer from a green tunnel
Sweet pickleheads stuffed in a jar.

He twists a small Allen wrench
Reaching up, perched
On his toolbox as
Small deft hands reach out, poised to help
Circling, searching for something
To touch, feel, hold or do,
A washer or perhaps a screw.

I'm gonna help
Knows what needs to be done
Tiny fingers grasp a nylon spacer
Her hair dangles down
Over the wrench turning in his hand.

Unconcerned playground monitors watch
Keeping more pickle-heads out of the jar.
I'm gonna help
Reminds him of a picture of his wife at her age
With her heart and spirit.

He does not know any of their parents
But in one sense he knows them deeply
They are good people.

Whatcha doin and his friend
Gonna be done by the second bell?
Stand below, curious, planning ahead,
Clear as glass.

Like the others they carry no facades yet
He looks into their eyes
And silently wishes them many years
He looks ahead twenty-five years and feels safe.

The Ashland City Band

Early evening young families gather on the park lawn
To picnic before the city band takes the stage
When children's eyes dart nervously at the multitude
Of smiling and wrinkled strangers on nylon chairs
And little hands cling to mom or dad with cares.

A hot August sun is passing and shadows stretch
Across perfectly trimmed and not quite dry grass
Prattling elders parade with friends in tow
To listen to Souza marches, anything else, Maestro?
Is it a medley or a melody? Oh how should I know!

Tuneless tuning of pipers and big bellied tuba players
Emit a cacophony of sound not meant for ears
On strolls the conductor whose confident pose
Stops the racket and he raises the baton with a proper 'ahem'
Children on shoulders are rising for the anthem.

With toe tapping marches the magic begins
They venture, first one, then two and now by dozens
Carried to the grass by small dancing feet
Runs, spins, strides and leaps cut the air
Eden's little lacewings at dusk neither alone nor in pairs.

Rhythmic old timers clapping hands or slapping thighs
Encourage the nymphs with twinkles in their eyes
Bold performers float in waves filling the air
Natural little choreographers with billowing dresses
Dazzle and sparkle with bouncing curls and tresses.

Far from the eye of sweeps dashing through the sky
Enveloped in an aura of sound and a synchronized crowd
They peak dramatically and then decrescendo
The sandman returns them to strong loving arms
Little spirits warmed by the Maestro and his charms.

Double Dog Dare Ya

Today is a time for leaping for joy!
And though it seems natural enough
For kids in caps and baby lambs
I must have put it off.
It's a skip, and I remember a klick,
But just because I can't say when
Doesn't mean I won't try it again
Cuz it's too much fun to waste on kids.
This morning I am going to check out
A truly great and mighty question:
Does joy leap for us
Or must we leap for joy?
Yeah ... and then I'm gonna laugh at you,
Because I'm never gonna tell
And you're never gonna know,
Unless there's a kid in your cap.

Bundled Up

Walking alone on the beach
I face directly into the wind, so
I'm swallowed by the roar
As I revel in natural wonders on the shore.

The beach is nearly bare, though
Sandpipers dart to retreating waves
Snatching morsels only to bound,
With fast jerky steps onto higher ground.

The winter storm pounds it's fury
Against ancient monoliths off the shore,
Frigid rain spatters my face as
Soaked feet plod and I lean to the brace.

Whiskers are erect on my cheeks
My chin is stiff as refrigerated meat
My jaw is clenched so my teeth ache
And cold ears scream for reason to take.

Here comes a dark squall about to pounce
I turn and follow my tracks in mottled sand.
Communing with nature makes me wiser
I'm buying a hat with flaps and a visor.

Distractions At The Comfort Inn

Hurling a star at Mach thirty-three
In a spin is important work
Requiring concentration, not unlike
Patting the head while rubbing the tummy,
So the hiss of cars and trucks
Scurrying down highway 97 distract and
Annoy me as do the scatter bursts of syllables
Of a staccato pitch-man in the room below
As he sells novitiates to Dream Americana how to,
My captured ears tune in
For the what, but alas without success.
Room service, push "0".
The irritating roadway sounds like
Ocean waves with back compression and brakes,
Only more hideous, it is us, evolutions current crown.
Wake up call, push "0".
South, a Yakima trucker hauling produce to LA
Caffeine in his blood and Rush in his ears
Week after bleary week, but North
Come rockin' two totally local dudes,
Brains toasting on blasts of cyberpunk,
Groins crawling with testosterone
Like dude, we need to move it cause
This is important shit dude
After sorry, we're gonna rule dude.
Message waiting, push "0".
East a woman in a shiny red Toyota
Pulls away from the fountain of youth gym
Aglow from the flow of adrenalin.
Try again, front desk, push "0".
South, a blissful dowager in gloves
Glides by silently in the center lane
Because she will turn left, or right
Whenever she finds
Whatever she wants wherever it is
If she remembers
And gawd-awfully slow
In the absolute confidence
Other drivers will not hit an old lady.

Local calls, push "8"
North, a roaring spray of hiss
Pursues a man with bulging veins
Powered by an addiction called rage
A curious habit that takes courage to fix.
Long distance, push "8 then 0".
From the East is Harry Honyocker
The muse, on his gaily painted bicycle
His orange and purple robes billowing
In the wind as he pedals to the setting Sun.
A convoy of cattle trucks
Pepper sand and mud at him and
Old Harry is not amused today
Total concentration is required
To guide the earth through space
At breakneck speeds in a spin.

Vivaldi After A Couple Scotches

Vivaldi remains a most interesting composer
His cascading first violins prancing like festooned ponies
Confident in the certainty they bear the children of kings
The good pleasure of royalty and cardinals his prolific command
The old red head, music teacher, priest, lover of young curls
Energetic full of vitality, naïve, prosaic and purposeful
He embroiders originals while scorning mediocrity
Melodic sopranos seem obedient slaves
To lower violas and baritone cellos
He was a clever fellow and I admire him.

First Time Buyer

He pours over maps looking for an American styled dream
Thought rich by many, but looking anywhere to find a house.
My keyboard clicks and we're oblivious to office noises
Punching up several neighborhoods we study the screens, select a few
Print, sort, route, call owners, get lost, lose key, break keypad
Fight to safely cross streets, drive by a few losers
I buy lunch and we explore more pages on the map
We pass over mistakes people corrected with more mistakes
We find a better route to an old part of town and exchange promises
To look elsewhere as we summarize the days lessons.

Half a dozen homes on a printout remain. We push through our fatigue.
I know the area is good and aim for one of the houses.
Perfect. We'll see it tomorrow.
It's almost as good as the first house he saw last week.
Same old curves but new to him.
Discovery is a required course. We do it his way.
Eighty miles of crazy cars and U-turns.

We're educated now. He knows a good value when he sees one.
I write his offer before he visits the house so it won't get away
No need for lessons I don't want to teach.   I need to move on.
I find myself building my business like I did before.
There must be a better way.

Beyond Today

What do you say
We look to the stars
For they shine
Above this abyss?

Seek something polar
Beyond today and wave after wave
Of sinking, rising and sinking again.

Tomorrow comes we can choose
A new interpretation
Demystifying by the light above.

Over hue and cry of arrows past
Let go the madness
Away brave people, away.

All We Like Sheep

An oracle falls from the lips of our leader
That the future of our great land can be found
Along the information highway
And no sooner is it said than done.
The image fans corporate imaginations and
Editors declare 'Whatever it is, write about it!'
In an instant techno god is born and
The earth groans under new maxims.
If something isn't broke, break it,
If conceived, it is passé.
If yet to be created, we need it yesterday.
The beast severs us from time and purpose.
Information highway with black holes? Techno cult?
Inquisitors on high hills beat drums,
I quake, afraid that a techno-god will
Stand and knock on my computer screen.
The babel shrieks like an infomercial
It is a noxious god, or so I say.
Will I confess my heretical ways?
Turn from the worm and the cheese?
I must go to work in the morning,
And return home at night, like always,
I mow the lawn and carry out the garbage,
I am not redeemed, yet believers abound.
The notion remains,
Separated people yearn for smiles.
Hearts beat to serve and be served,
Can they stay the empty road to Babylon?

History and great minds not long ago
Recorded compelling images of their time,
Of a country with character, values and utility.
I shall reach them on the internet.

TESTOSTERONE HAPPENS

My Sordid Affair

She wore the faintest of smiles
As our eyes met, but then it faded
When I pretended I had not noticed.
A mean gender specific payback
She did not deserve, a lovely person
No, she was stunningly beautiful
So even a faithful happy husband
Would be caught by her smile.

As my heartbeat slowed a bit
I planned an innocent maneuver
That would give me a better glimpse
At the tall, slender, incredible goddess
But before I picked a vantage point
She wheeled around the corner
We exchanged surprised looks and smiles
I fancied it as a peek into her soul
A flirting gift to me and I felt good.

She moved with grace like a queen
Through her royal court, so sure,
And for a moment I saw myself
As a courtesan and not the fool
I was therefore amazed my fantasy
Did not end because I saw her again,
And again and yet again, till she
Caught me squeezing mangoes.

We don't know each other, never met
I'm sure it was a chance encounter
With someone I must have loved
Could have loved or would have loved.
I should claim it's evidence
Of other lifetimes, or more poetically
That like little butterflies, we are drawn
Irresistibly to the most spectacular blooms.

The whole affair was over in minutes
There were no words or silly advances
She was a lovely person dear and,
I promise I'll never see her again.
One more time: I'll never
Go shopping at Safeway again.

The Man From The Fourth Street Florist

Let me tell you about Gene
Whose life intersected
Briefly with mine
In the early nineties in Southern Oregon.
Who bought a house from my friend Deane,
When he became
The chief administrator
At a hospital called Providence,
Operated by Catholic sisters.
Someone in the office whispered,
I think he's gay, surely
The sisters would have to know it, wouldn't they?
Oh, they don't care, offered another
All they want is a good administrator.
I recall Gene as bright and cheerful
So slim In his tight blue jeans
This gay guy,
And he always had a smile
On his face when he came
To see my friend Deane
But as time went by I could see
He was sick and one day
My dear friend Deane told me
He was dying of AIDS.
He quit his important job
To do what he always dreamed of doing
And so he worked in a florist's shop
Down on Fourth Street.
I thought he would be good at that.

Gene had my pal Deane sell his house
And buy him a little townhouse
Because it was easier
To take care of and he made arrangements
To give it to his sister
When he was gone.
I remember thinking he was a nice man
And though I felt compassion for him

I forgot about this
Slim forty-five year old man
And moved on with my work.
I didn't really know him personally
Except through my friend Deane
And then my wife told me one night
Over dinner
She had met this really nice man
At the Fourth Street Florist
Who understood what she wanted
To hang over the Kimono
When she waved her arms with a swish
Which she did for me
Though I had no idea what
She wanted to hang
On the living room wall.
She said he had already been to our house
To look at the wall.
She also said he recognized my picture
On the piano and I said
That must be Gene,
He's a really nice man, very talented
And a friend of my friend Deane
Who quit a high powered job
At the Sisters of Providence
To work as a flower arranger
But at the time I did not tell her
He was sick.
In a couple of days Gene delivered
A beautiful sash with huge
Dried Peace Roses among others
And a gorgeous crepe bow
Fastened to a long bundle of grape vines
That had an oriental flair and it said 'swish'
Just like when she waved her arms
Which delighted her and she said
Isn't that amazing
How he made that?
She said he liked our home so well
That he made a little gift
For us.

In a burnished clay pot
He erected side by side
Two small bundles of willow twigs
To which he tied two smaller
Horizontal bundles of twigs,
And onto this lovely grid
He then fastened seven dried roses.
Like the others
They were beautiful and enhanced
The look Suzanne wanted.
My story takes it's inevitable turn
As you might expect
Because a few months later
My sad friend Deane came to the office
And said Gene had died
I felt compassion for her but I
Continued with my work.
A few weeks later there was an estate sale
Advertised among the many garage sales
Which Suzanne called to my attention
Because we needed this, that,
And the other thing,
Especially two chairs and a table.
I told her it was at Gene's house
And that Deane
Said to go early because
He had many wonderful things
That would go quickly.
When I arrived at the estate sale
At ten in the morning I was greeted
By sold stickers
Bearing the name Suzanne
I loaded the things she bought
And dawdling around the house
I found two books
That sounded interesting at the time:
I wonder what this wonderful man
Hoped to find in them.

The Right Use of Will, healing and evolving
The emotional body and
The Miracle of Mindfulness
By the Buddhist monk named Thich Nhat Hahn
Which I bought for fifty cents each.
Gene had been a real person to me but
Now even the common things in his home
Seemed to point at the fact life
Can be short and it is sacred
I was saddened for the people
Who loved him: A mom and dad,
A sister.
Looking through the kitchen
I saw wine glasses and
I imagined the lover who died first
Had bravely toasted Gene
'To health and to happiness'.
This was all several years ago
And we have moved since.
My daughter reupholstered the two chairs
And today my accounting is spread all over
Genes table.
The burnished pot sits on top
Of a bookshelf
And the sash that goes swish
Is over the head of our bed
Because our new living room ceiling is too low
For it to be placed above the Kimono.
I read the books but for some reason
They seemed inconsequential to me
At least compared to his life.
The table and the beautiful things he made
Remind me how in unexpected ways
Our lives intersected with a man named Gene
And a dear lady named Deane.
The books bother me because
I know what I go through to select a book,
He probably struggled with his
Decisions as well.

111

Of Course I Can

Change anytime I want.
A little delusion wrapped in a grin,
But oh durable one,
You haven't changed a bit.
A bit of truth here,
I wish you would.
And the illusion I can
Sticks with me like sugar baked on a spoon
In this swirl of life, however erratic,
I change to adapt
Or react---whatever.
But change for change sake? Never!
Like a cat into a rat? No.
Even as I speak
Six billion of me navigate some stage of illusion
The sands of youth slip the fingers,
Slow as a lichen eating a rock; but today
Faster than an antelope on an ill wind.
The view from today is different
Than the certainty of then,
Everything changes, yet nothing
Life cycle stuff, I suppose
I wear spandex and will exercise
Till I become a museum piece, hollow and fragile
I skip the moment to cheat the future.
Change my hat, change my age
Change my mind, even my sight,
But I endure as a constant
In a time capsule I call me.

Snapdragons

They come blooming when others go
Colorfully leading and quite the show
Snapdragons, full grown and illustrious
On soil red, warmed from injustice.

Offering hope in hopeless lands,
The bud of freedom in their hands
Ground seized for one and for all,
Held by one who ignores the call.

No smile, now turn, devouring their own,
Predators different from those I've know
Facing final challenges on shaky old frames
Through benign looking smiles, parades and games

Repeating patterns and snuffing cries
Their children's children before my eyes
Till others shaken as the madness grows
Finally come, crouching young lions, heroes.

Perhaps innocent like myself and green
I see the moment as through a screen
Now smile, now turn and carry the flag on,
Yes I'm the seed of another snapdragon.

Tiananmen Square
June 11, 1989

113

Hearing Voices

Awake 0 nation, Can't you see
The clear threat to your liberty
Here! Now! In our yard!
Let's call up the National Guard.
Where Great Father I can't see
There's a threat to my liberty?
What can I do? Where can I go?
Say, weren't you on the late, late show?
The nations at risk, it's plain to see
There's an enemy behind every tree.
I'll call the Army; I'll call the Guard
I'll throw the leftists from your yard.
Create Great Father as you please
Much Madison Avenue diplomacy.
Tell me again, who shall I hate?
I want your truth to propagate.
Evil Empires I will attack
Both hands tied behind my back.
Freedom Fighters! Cheer! Cheer! Cheer!
I'll keep you safe in the hemisphere.
Thanks Great Father, now I see
There was a threat to my liberty.
Protect our honor, protect our pride
But keep my eyes from the genocide.
Awake 0 Nation, there's a war,
A bloody, boastful, bloated whore.
Public diplomat, tell me again
Why's my country slaughtering the poor?

Old Dog Dreams

I wish I could meet him face to face
So I can put the war behind me
And stop the war within me
That began seventy years ago.

I want to make my own declaration of peace
Then there will be a cessation of hostility
And perhaps, just perhaps, the fury within me
Will become a flame of peace.

For the sake of my sorry soul.
I say we meet on neutral ground
Neither here nor there
So there is an equal footing,

I extend my hand to him
We acknowledgements and recognition
We exchange thin smiles
And bow.

It would be a ceremony of sorts.
So I can put the war behind me
Stop the weary war within me
That weary, old war.

The Difference

The winner and still champion
Whose outstretched fist
Stretched out the foe
That closed the eye
Which had not seen but sensed
A blow that made the difference

Rehearsed alone
When others had gone
With desire matched with discipline
Heart beyond mind
Courage past limits
Yet he had foreseen
The moment that made the difference

The mighty roar
Did not still the voice
Speaking the lonely truth
That preparation
Had delivered
The moment, the blow and yes
The luck that made the difference.

Pretenders

As much gray matter as Old John had
In, between and upon his ears,
He talked all his four and ninety years
About problems he would fix
If he were the mayor, governor, president
Or maybe even God.
That would be nice, said I,
And at age eight I knew he'd make
A fine president because
He smoked White Owl cigars, iced his Jim Crow
And carried himself with poise.
He was an important man,
Though the gutters on his house
Caught winged maple seeds
That grew into a tiny forest.
And though tall bluegrass waved
From his yard like politicians in a parade,
Old John concerned himself with
Public life and dynamic issues of the day.

Myself, I had the misfortune
To fall in with Wes Turleblow
Easily as smart as Old John
Wes could get into any business deal,
And could be often seen at the city gates
Taking bold dynamic action.
He could not however get out of these deals
Whence it took years of my life to get free,
But before then I noticed my dog Jake
Would run boldly, act dynamically
And pose proudly upon a hillock,
Where he too could be seen by all.
Like Jake, Wes was a con man,
Unlike Jake he drank single malt Scotch
And unlike John he smoked fine cigars.
In western boots his tall frame
With a Stetson on top looked the part.

Wes could brilliantly assess the venality
Of every petty pol in town, and more
If only he knew an ax handle from
A horse's tail about business.

Roanoke Ripped as a boy
Said the world's nuclear arsenal
Would blow up the whole planet,
And he was smart enough to say no.
It did not matter anyway,
His litanies to his friends,
No to sports, no to school,
No to scouts, no to family,
No to skills, no to job exploitation.
He would not be taken by the system.
With smoke as his ally he is
Organically enlightened and
Might be seen outside grocery stores near you
Boldly signing petitioners to free hemp
Boasting he does not pollute his mind
Or read newspapers.

And so it was an old man, a young man, and a boy
Like my dog shared a flair for style,
Living colorful lives by pretending;
And surrounding themselves
With people who let them pretend.

A Man Turns Sixty

The small man in black could have been
A poorly dressed Hackman
Tending a horse and cab
In the nineteenth century.
He was, however, an usher to the birth
Of a new millennia,
He is out of place, but he could be
A misfit in any time.
He wears heavy, plastic glasses,
Dark pants and a black trench coat
His hair is slick with Brylcream
And his feet are shod in rubber soles.
He's a sixty year old boom baby in lockstep,
He loves chicks, cars and classic rock
Who says when he was in Nam
He sharpened a very angry edge.
Today he barks out his life in decades
His fist shaking defiantly,
At me, as if I'm father time:
The sixties are mine! All mine!

If You Were From Mars

If you were from Mars I would say
Hey: Mikhailov! Let's start at the beginning
Let's talk rock and roll
You may not know Bruce Springsteen
As well as the Moscow Ballet but
Please don't think we have lost our way
So soon barely being in our mid sixties
I will say hey! It's better late
Than not at all and growing up
On the prairie coyotes cackling
To the golden moon on snow glazed nights
Lawrence Welk left champagne music flat
Our main juice was the Cavaliers
High School guys who formed a band
And Elvis was king and so we roamed

Country roads with girlfriends looking
For a nice place to neck, say Hey!
Maybe John Denver thought it up
In the back seat of his dad's car
Rocky Mountain High wasn't till
Viet Nam was almost over.
And then we got married just kids
Humping and having kids while Bruce
Was just getting started
Veritas Hayseed that old goat
Put it to me this way say hey!
I was forty when I was born
With liver spots on thin white skin
Sporting velvet an blue gray hair
Drinking Coke and eating cookies

At school picnics while bigger guys
Ate red slabs of watermelons
Juice on their chins and farm tans
But Mikhailov I digress
I went to see what all the fuss
Was about I didn't know
Bruce Springsteen from an Evinrude
Though similarities exist
I am sure, and differences too
The ruckus had been about us
And attitude was important

As apple pie and motherhood
So when Suzanne proposed that we

120

See Springsteen at his reunion
With the latter day E Street Band
Cobbled together one more time
I say, Say Hey! it sounds like fun
It seemed the chance of a lifetime
To rock with roots I never had
To relive some saccharine youth
Or misty moment till our eardrums burst
Tell me about Tatiana
Veritas Hayseed that old goat
Thought it a good way to blow dough
And sitting in the cupola
Of the arena I agreed
When ten thousand sand we want Boo
I admit to moments of doubt
But standing in the beer garden
Before the concert was a kick.

As thousands milled about
Sporting tee shirts and old sweaters
From previous Springsteen concerts
Craning to find old college friends
We were trucker, cops and robbers
Stock brokers, plumbers and bureaucrats
So for an instant we were one
United without avarice
Or the corrosive quirks of time
A bit I would say like heaven
Full of strangers I might have know
Igor your silence concerns me
When you don't answer my emails.

Your last trip to America
You tried to buy Tamoxifen
Panic set your jaw when money
Could not buy Tatiana time
Say Hey, What do you think of Bruce?
In the cupola I wondered
If the scalper might have scalped us
The crowd now roiling for Boo Boo
Veritas Hayseed smiled to say
I think we got on the wrong bus.

Psychedelic Seeing Eye dogs
With tie-died collars seem retro
Tomorrow comes and we'll be deaf
Just like the man in the beer line
Who, if I could read sign correctly,

Said the man from Jersey who flew in
To attend his eighty-eighth
Bruce Springsteen concert, don't you know.
My parents think I'm off the edge
Splat! It is my big birthday so
Mellow dude, what was their first clue?
Then the music began Igor
The crowd rockin', and swaying weird
For people my age is seemed queer
Then I remembered what I missed
Senility is why I'm here
In a cupola with Bruce below
Veritas Hayseed said Say Hey!
Remember you were born forty
When forty meant you was nothing.
You and Tatiana moved out
To the country for healthy air
I fear it will take more than air.

But you did what you both thought best.
Congratulations by the way
Your crazy president now pickled and gone
But ours still prances
In the public eye and I suspect your spies
Have heard a saxophone cry
All the way from the Washington monument
I do think Clarence of Bruce's band
Did the low mournful notes so much better.
Say Hey! Old Veritas Hayseed
Went to the music store and bought
Bruce Springsteen and the E Street Band
If you were born forty as I you may
As well been from Mars I would say.

The Deal

Ever at my side,
Nose against toes,
Bored and omnipresent
Heaving an occasional sigh.

I think he loves me,
If only incidentally,
Because I feed him
Treats, like occasional biscuits.

It is an exchange of sorts,
I let him out and in again,
And he doesn't piss on the floor,
But lies at my feet.

Silly Season Frames

Silly season calls for thinking
Sifting truth from fiction without blinking
As if truth does not perish when
Posers, liars and breathless anchors

Fray the ties that bind as we
'Forward all' the lies never mind
Letters and words falling swords
Whisper campaigns severed cords.

Some say this discourse is fair
Advancing the cause good citizens declare
Left or right all framing a vision
Song-birds muted notes hidden.

Sound bites for the sloshed or sloth
Dog whistles connecting the thoughtless
Silly season is time to consider
Who gains, loses or is the highest bidder.

Silly season is no cottage industry
Big business year round and blustery
Lies framing our minds
Driving wedges unworthy unkind.

One nation divisible after all
Misplaced trust so when we fall
We 'Forward All' rotting from within
Thus silly season includes chagrin.

Polarized lacking skills to trust or talk
Listen then listen again raising no block
If discussed thoughtfully one can find
A new frame and common state of mind.

SPIRITUAL ECHOES

The Sabbath

It was a Sunday morning fire drill by God
Every week and all of us stood together.
Jesus stood in our mad, mad midst, for,
Jesus Christ! Who took the comb?

I can't find my other sock. Mom!
Kathy took my sock. We're late and
Not by fate but St. Christopher and a
Wide-eyed plastic Jesus did we arrive safely.

And it was hilarious to watch the spit wash
Of a grubby little brood
By mom in her hat as we clocked Dad in
The Ford covering five miles in three minutes.

Not bad! Can't hear crinkling candy wrappers
Reciting, Et cum spiritu tuo. Get me to grandma's
Cinnamon rolls. Ho Ho Holy Holy
Get me to grandpa's Benedicat vos.

Cousins, aunts, uncles, everybody's there.
Card games a goin'. Pull up a chair.
A game from hell, full house. Jesus! Shut the door.
Laughter, smoke, Damn. Could you ask for more?

Mea maxima culpa!

Storm

My feet and head rub the arms of the couch
As I drift between sleep and the anticipation
Some internal alarm was set to ring
Telling me to rise and catch the plane,
That would return me to the present and another place
I have known for most of my life, and so away
From my past gathered yesterday in reunion.
The past my present has crossed my face.
Then came a rumble. Old Thor is bored, roaming this slice
Of life trying to thrive on the Great Plains; and now
He's calling his children to distant times, and promising
Eternal sights, and smells and sounds that splice.
I remember and stir in the dark as the advancing strains
Announce the roaring god in the fast, flashy chariot.
Riotously closing this reunion for me while making
Chase in his race with a hundred furious trains.
Marvelously his roaring display chased toward the unseen sun
Leaving in its wake old thrills and a moment of wonder:
Dare I confront him or shall I just leap aboard?
Still blessed as child of the plain, loved and having fun.
I pause now, savoring the moment, looking back
Many years and I'm joined by a realization the people
Who have passed, are now and who will be
All share the revealed as if a bush on another tract.
Thor had thundered on but could still be heard, so
I tie my shoes in darkness, some ambivalence gone,
Stuffing my bags into a rented car I inhale the storm
That had left water, fresh air, and ozone without a scar.
The elemental time faded on Interstate-Twenty-Nine
And died in the exhaust of jet fuel, while I,
Seated between strangers in a world between airports,
Struggled to reconcile the malignant and benign.
From the window I see distant clouds running like a whelp,
That had at once addressed me as infinitely important
And utterly without importance; and I am left to wonder
If I AM WITH YOU ALWAYS is always there to help.

Certainty Lost

Like a stream of fine lines from a single
Vanishing point a powerful argument
Can sweep me into its brilliance, and momentarily
I am dazzled by the certainty of it all

An arrogant hold, a grip with bravado
That however myopic, has the numbing
Effect of comfort standing guard
To an array of unexamined half-baked views

The original breach is a flawed mindset
Admitting one fuzzy thought, then another
Till a habit of relativity seizes me, surrounding me
In a spherical and debilitating web of possibilities

A sorry symmetry of ideas, paralyzing one another
In a bath of equality and indecision, till
Without the safety of conviction, I am alone
In a quiet thoughtful abyss.

Earth Climber

I ascend from red stardust alone
Pink and smooth, wet with clay
Mother dances, animals sing
Fields are plowed, trees are planted.

The earth tells me I am not alone
Warm showers scrub me
Tall thick and green, deer browse and leap
Strawberries grow on her breast.

I ascend to the trees alone
Ruddy lean and strong
Birds fly through my fingers and hair
Fruit emerges from my body.

I ascend blue foothills alone
Now bronzed rough to the core
Bears strip my leggings, rub my trunk
I offer the earth veined leaves.

I ascend the mountain alone
Mottled gray, Zephyr bowed
An eagle claims a snag near me
This is as far as I go, he says.

I start for the summit alone
Snow and clouds drift around me
From below mother dances, animals sing
Vermillion feet stain the snow.

Gentle Vision

Stay open gentle vision
Creamy flowers of embryonic
Hands, buds, fingers, petals
Let me see again
Your dicot seed
Unfold and open into whorl after whorl
Of little palms
Reaching heavenward on ivory stems.

Stems of tenderness
Rising and waving in gentle breeze
Fingers unfolding
Releasing more tiny hands
Opening palms
And fingers in dreamy attitudes
Morphing the language of hands
Into supplicating hands
Serving hands
Loving fingers
Fleshy promises.

A promise of innocence floating aloft
As if long strings of balloons touching the sky
Stay open gentle vision
Bring more beauty
I will wait and wonder
From whence you came
And what you mean.

Novel But Was It A Crime?

He came as himself
Without obvious facades
He wasn't just anybody
So maybe he really was God.

Had no tribal costume
And he didn't have a crest
He sounded authentic and people listened
He came dressed as himself.

Didn't come as a member
Of a party, church or state
He came as himself
Hard to imagine he was great.

He was not overbearing
He really wasn't a ham
He was best at who he was
As I am who I am.

His authority made people mad
Spoke out without invective
He seemed interested in us and
More transparent than reflective.

Times wobble but someday may bring
Clarity over a foggy climb
Who was he really, because he was
Novel but was it a crime?

The Rebel

He chooses to find his way from within
The obscurity and fog of uncertainty
He forsakes question-less living
He frequents the haunts of ethereal answers
He ignores the hard rock in his shoe

From reflection seeking meaning
Insights and wisdom
He finds only sound-bites
Starlight, foolishness and odd foreign coins.

Lost in a gray mist
This rebel on a pale Burren
Is cold and alone
Still robed in the sheepish grin
A mystic in his wet shroud.

In desperation he quits the role of being wise
He seeks God directly
God who laughs out loud and
Holds the rebel in a net.
A rebel helpless as a hare in a snare.

Softies

We are dreamers
Holding to a world of our own
We are gentle, whether big or small
We are love.
We are encouragers
Offering kindness to everyone
Though we know few will dance
We are love.
We are healers
Making people whole if we can
Some cannot comprehend our game
Because we are not naive.
We are different
Loving because it is our call
We know fear keeps them in their cell
And they have to hate.
We are not focused
Except that we obey the call
Enduring at times heat and ridicule
Because we love.
We are softies
Stopping often to enjoy the blooms
Very aware there's work undone
Always time to love.
We love the thing that is beautiful
Whether in people, songs or sights
We realize all life is of value to us and
Worthy of love.
How we live our days
Some see as quite a waste
They are troubled and deeply suspicious
Of love as a genuine motive.
We are the risk takers
Betting throughout our lives
That our strategy will lead to others
Who are love.
You see, we are love
Life and God has made it so,
How can our mission be so vital
That we love our foe?

I've been told it makes no sense
Though I never said it did.
We have always been around and
None will change their bid.
We are kind creatures
We love others and can be oblivious
Outside forces manage to shield us
Who forget to protect ourselves.

What To Expect

In the time remaining before the lion lies down with the lamb
I expect to walk for miles on the shore alone,
To explore the litter and littoral, at my own pace
Just as I expect to explore museums by myself,
At my own pace. No one would be bothered
If I thoroughly and slowly took it all in.

In the time remaining I expect to be the lion of my life
The leader, crouching, breathing quietly
Waiting, then exploding to the kill
Afterwards flopping in cool shade for a nap.
Likewise I am the lamb of my life, a member of the flock,
A follower, a creamy suckling, pure and soft.

In the time remaining before they lie down together as dust
I will honor life, sip and sample the universe
Know fortune and grief to the capacity of my being.
I expect to live being full and being empty
To love, to take my time, to read to someone who cannot
And discover the truth about the universe from children.

In the time remaining this is what I expect.
In the time remaining.